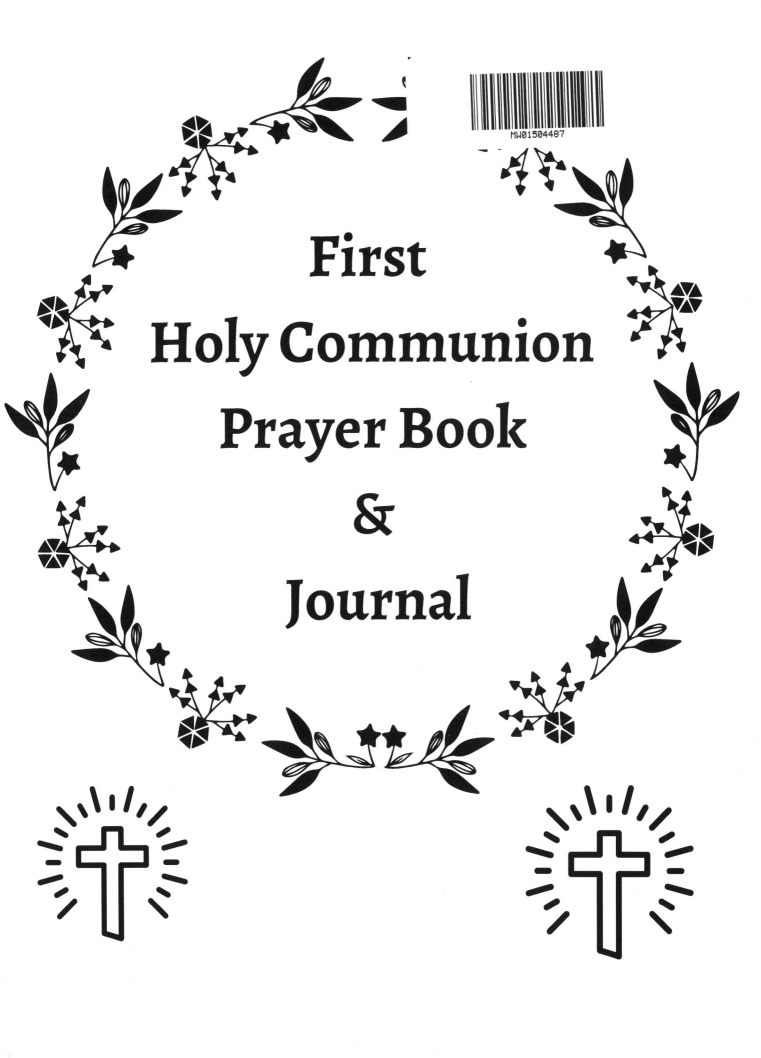

First
Holy Communion
Prayer Book
&
Journal

Name

_____

_____

Date of Ceremony _____

Place _____

Time _____

Prayer Index

The Sign of the Cross

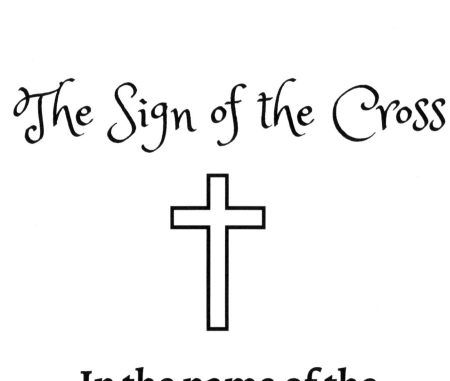

**In the name of the
Father,
and of the
Son, and
of the Holy Spirit.
Amen.**

The Lord's Prayer

**Our Father,
who art in heaven,
hallowed be thy name;
thy Kingdom come;
thy will be done on earth
as it is in heaven.
Give us this day our daily bread;
and
forgive us our trespasses
as we forgive
those who trespass against us;
and lead us not into temptation
but
deliver us from evil.
Amen.**

The Hail Mary

**Hail Mary,
full of grace,
the Lord is with you;
blessed are you among women,
and blessed is the fruit of your womb, Jesus.
Holy Mary, Mother of God,
pray for us sinners,
now and at the hour of our death.
Amen.**

Glory Be to

Glory be to the Father,
and to the Son
and
to the Holy Spirit.
As it was in the beginning,
is now, and ever shall be;
world without end.
Amen.

The Penitential Rite

I confess to almighty God and to you,
my brothers and sisters,
that I have greatly sinned,
in my thoughts and in my words,
in what I have done
and in what I have failed to do,
(and, striking their breast, they say:)
through my fault,
through my fault,
through my most grievous fault;
therefore I ask Blessed Mary ever-Virgin,
all the Angels and Saints,
and you,
my brothers and sisters,
to pray for me to the Lord our God.

The Gloria

Glory to God in the highest,
and on earth peace to people of good will.
We praise you,
we bless you, we adore you, we glorify you,
we give you thanks for your great glory,
Lord God, heavenly King, O God, almighty Father.
Lord Jesus Christ,
Only Begotten Son, Lord God, Lamb of God,
Son of the Father,
you take away the sins of the world,
have mercy on us;
you take away the sins of the world,
receive our prayer;
you are seated at the right hand of the Father,
have mercy on us.
For you alone are the Holy One,
you alone are the Lord,
you alone are the Most High,
Jesus Christ,
with the Holy Spirit,
in the glory of God the Father. Amen.

The Apostles' Creed

I believe in God,
the Father Almighty,
Creator of heaven and earth,
and in Jesus Christ, his only Son, our Lord,
(At the words that follow up to
and including the virgin Mary,
all bow.)
who was conceived by the
Holy Spirit,
born of the Virgin Mary,
suffered under Pontius Pilate,
was crucified, died and was buried;
he descended into hell;
on the third day he rose again from the dead;
he ascended into heaven,
and is seated at the right hand of God
the Father Almighty;
from there he will come to judge the living and the dead.
I believe in the Holy Spirit, the holy catholic Church,
the communion of saints,
the forgiveness of sins,
the resurrection of the body,
and life everlasting. Amen.

Act Of Contrition

Act of Contrition (short form)

O my God, I am sorry for all my sins,
because they displease You,
Who are All-good and deserving of all my love.
With Your help, I will sin no more.

Act of Contrition
O my God,
I am heartily sorry for having offended Thee,
and I detest all my sins
because of thy just punishments,
but most of all because they offend Thee,
my God,
who art all good and deserving of all my love.
I firmly resolve with the help of
Thy grace to sin no more
and to avoid the near occasion of sin. Amen.

Grace before Meals

**Bless us,
O Lord, and these Your gifts,
which we are about to
receive from Your bounty,
through Christ our Lord. Amen.**

Grace after Meals

**We give You thanks,
almighty God,
for these and all the benefits
which we have received from
Your bounty,
through Christ our Lord.
Amen.**

BIBLICAL

MANDALA

Prayers for Family and Friends

Prayers for Family and Friends

_____

_____

_____

_____

_____

_____

_____

_____

_____

_____

_____

Prayers for Family and Friends

_____

_____

_____

_____

_____

_____

_____

_____

_____

_____

_____

Prayers for Family and Friends

_____

_____

_____

_____

_____

_____

_____

_____

_____

_____

_____

_____

Prayers for Family and Friends

_____

_____

_____

_____

_____

_____

_____

_____

_____

_____

_____

Prayers for Family and Friends

_____

_____

_____

_____

_____

_____

_____

_____

_____

_____

_____

_____

Prayers for Family and Friends

_____

_____

_____

_____

_____

_____

_____

_____

_____

_____

_____

Prayers for Family and Friends

_____

_____

_____

_____

_____

_____

_____

_____

_____

_____

_____

Prayers for Family and Friends

_____

_____

_____

_____

_____

_____

_____

_____

_____

_____

_____

Prayers for Family and Friends

_____

_____

_____

_____

_____

_____

_____

_____

_____

_____

_____

Prayers for Family and Friends

_____

_____

_____

_____

_____

_____

_____

_____

_____

_____

_____

Prayers for Family and Friends

_____

_____

_____

_____

_____

_____

_____

_____

_____

_____

_____

Prayers for Family and Friends

_____

_____

_____

_____

_____

_____

_____

_____

_____

_____

_____

_____

Prayers for Family and Friends

_____

_____

_____

_____

_____

_____

_____

_____

_____

_____

_____

_____

Prayers for Family and Friends

_____

_____

_____

_____

_____

_____

_____

_____

_____

_____

_____

_____

Prayers for Family and Friends

_____

_____

_____

_____

_____

_____

_____

_____

_____

_____

_____

_____

Prayers for Family and Friends

_____

_____

_____

_____

_____

_____

_____

_____

_____

_____

_____

_____

Prayers for Family and Friends

_____

_____

_____

_____

_____

_____

_____

_____

_____

_____

_____

_____

Prayers for Family and Friends

_____

_____

_____

_____

_____

_____

_____

_____

_____

_____

_____

Prayers for Family and Friends

_____

_____

_____

_____

_____

_____

_____

_____

_____

_____

_____

Prayers for Family and Friends

_____

_____

_____

_____

_____

_____

_____

_____

_____

_____

_____

_____

Bible Study

Today's Bible Study
For Kids

Today's Verse

What I'm Thankful For:

My Prayer Today:

What Today's Verse Taught Me:

Today's Bible Study
For Kids

Today's Verse

What I'm Thankful For:

My Prayer Today:

What Today's Verse Taught Me:

Today's Bible Study
For Kids

Today's Verse

What I'm Thankful For:

My Prayer Today:

What Today's Verse Taught Me:

Today's Bible Study
For Kids

Today's Verse

What I'm Thankful For:

My Prayer
Today:

What Today's Verse
Taught Me:

Today's Bible Study
For Kids

Today's Verse

What I'm Thankful For:

My Prayer Today:

What Today's Verse Taught Me:

Today's Bible Study
For Kids

Today's Verse

What I'm Thankful For:

My Prayer Today:

What Today's Verse Taught Me:

Today's Bible Study
For Kids

Today's Verse

What I'm Thankful For:

My Prayer Today:

What Today's Verse Taught Me:

Today's Bible Study
For Kids

Today's Verse

What I'm Thankful For:

My Prayer Today:

What Today's Verse Taught Me:

Today's Bible Study
For Kids

Today's Verse

What I'm Thankful For:

My Prayer Today:

What Today's Verse Taught Me:

Today's Bible Study
For Kids

Today's Verse

What I'm Thankful For:

My Prayer Today:

What Today's Verse Taught Me:

Today's Bible Study
For Kids

Today's Verse

What I'm Thankful For:

My Prayer Today:

What Today's Verse Taught Me:

Today's Bible Study
For Kids

Today's Verse

What I'm Thankful For:

My Prayer
Today:

What Today's Verse
Taught Me:

Today's Bible Study
For Kids

Today's Verse

What I'm Thankful For:

My Prayer
Today:

What Today's Verse
Taught Me:

Today's Bible Study
For Kids

Today's Verse

What I'm Thankful For:

My Prayer Today:

What Today's Verse Taught Me:

Today's Bible Study
For Kids

Today's Verse

What I'm Thankful For:

My Prayer Today:

What Today's Verse Taught Me:

Today's Bible Study
For Kids

Today's Verse

What I'm Thankful For:

My Prayer
Today:

What Today's Verse
Taught Me:

Today's Bible Study
For Kids

Today's Verse

What I'm Thankful For:

My Prayer Today:

What Today's Verse Taught Me:

Today's Bible Study
For Kids

Today's Verse

What I'm Thankful For:

My Prayer
Today:

What Today's Verse
Taught Me:

Today's Bible Study
For Kids

Today's Verse

What I'm Thankful For:

My Prayer Today:

What Today's Verse Taught Me:

Today's Bible Study
For Kids

Today's Verse

What I'm Thankful For:

My Prayer Today:

What Today's Verse Taught Me:

Today's Bible Study
For Kids

Today's Verse

What I'm Thankful For:

My Prayer Today:

What Today's Verse Taught Me:

Today's Bible Study
For Kids

Today's Verse

What I'm Thankful For:

My Prayer Today:

What Today's Verse Taught Me:

Today's Bible Study
For Kids

Today's Verse

What I'm Thankful For:

My Prayer Today:

What Today's Verse Taught Me:

Today's Bible Study
For Kids

Today's Verse

What I'm Thankful For:

My Prayer Today:

What Today's Verse Taught Me:

Today's Bible Study
For Kids

Today's Verse

What I'm Thankful For:

My Prayer Today:

What Today's Verse Taught Me:

Today's Bible Study
For Kids

Today's Verse

What I'm Thankful For:

My Prayer Today:

What Today's Verse Taught Me:

Today's Bible Study
For Kids

Today's Verse

What I'm Thankful For:

My Prayer Today:

What Today's Verse Taught Me:

Today's Bible Study
For Kids

Today's Verse

What I'm Thankful For:

My Prayer Today:

What Today's Verse Taught Me:

Today's Bible Study
For Kids

Today's Verse

What I'm Thankful For:

My Prayer Today:

What Today's Verse Taught Me:

Today's Bible Study
For Kids

Today's Verse

What I'm Thankful For:

My Prayer
Today:

What Today's Verse
Taught Me:

My Thoughts

My Thoughts

_____

_____

_____

_____

_____

_____

_____

_____

_____

_____

_____

_____

_____

_____

_____

_____

_____

_____

My Thoughts

_____

_____

_____

_____

_____

_____

_____

_____

_____

_____

_____

_____

_____

_____

_____

My Thoughts

_____

_____

_____

_____

_____

_____

_____

_____

_____

_____

_____

_____

_____

_____

_____

_____

My Thoughts

My Thoughts

My Thoughts

My Thoughts

My Thoughts

My Thoughts

_____

_____

_____

_____

_____

_____

_____

_____

_____

_____

_____

_____

_____

_____

_____

_____

_____

My Thoughts

My Thoughts

My Thoughts

My Thoughts

My Thoughts

My Thoughts

My Thoughts

_____

_____

_____

_____

_____

_____

_____

_____

_____

_____

_____

_____

_____

_____

My Thoughts

My Thoughts

My Thoughts

My Thoughts

My Thoughts

My Thoughts

My Thoughts

_____

_____

_____

_____

_____

_____

_____

_____

_____

_____

_____

_____

_____

_____

_____

_____

My Thoughts

My Thoughts

My Thoughts

_____

_____

_____

_____

_____

_____

_____

_____

_____

_____

_____

_____

_____

_____

My Thoughts

My Thoughts

My Thoughts

My Thoughts

My Thoughts

My Thoughts

My Thoughts

My Thoughts

My Thoughts

My Thoughts

My Thoughts

My Thoughts

My Thoughts

_____

_____

_____

_____

_____

_____

_____

_____

_____

_____

_____

_____

_____

_____

_____

_____

My Thoughts

My Thoughts

My Thoughts

My Thoughts

My Thoughts

My Thoughts

_____

_____

_____

_____

_____

_____

_____

_____

_____

_____

_____

_____

_____

_____

_____

Made in United States
Orlando, FL
28 April 2025

60866027R00074